TIME FOR CLOCKS

Daphne and John Trivett

Pictures by Giulio Maestro

THOMAS Y. CROWELL · NEW YORK

by Daphne Harwood Trivett

Shadow Geometry

by John V. Trivett

Building Tables on Tables:
A Book about Multiplication

For Joslyn, Erica and Lesley

Library of Congress Cataloging in Publication Data

Trivett, Daphne.   Time for clocks
SUMMARY: Provides instructions for several easy-to-
make clocks that demonstrate the concept of time.
1. Time—Juvenile literature. 2. Clocks and
watches—Juvenile literature. [1. Time. 2. Clocks
and watches] I. Trivett, John, joint
author. II. Maestro, Giulio, ill. III. Title.
QB209.5.T74 1979   529   78-4782
ISBN 0-690-03896-8 lib. bdg.
First Edition

TIME FOR CLOCKS

Once upon a time, before there were clocks, people told the time by the sun. You can, too!

Think of the sun in the sky at different times between sunup and sundown. Can you tell where it will be when you get up, have breakfast, go to school, have lunch, come home from school, go to bed?

Does the sun go from your left to your right, or the opposite way?

When will it be at its highest in the sky?

When will it look its largest?

Do you think the sun really comes up, or does the earth go down?

Is it the sun that moves?

You can make a sundial in your backyard. Place a stick upright in the ground and watch its shadow at different times during one day.

Put stones at the end of the shadows—one when you get up, another at breakfast time... and so on, until sundown.

Were the spaces between your stones equal? Would they be the same if you started all over again and made a new sundial tomorrow?

Watching the sun or the shadows the sun casts is a crude way to tell time. Long ago, people put numbers on sundials to make them a little more exact.

But a sundial is not very useful on a cloudy day when there are no shadows. You can't carry one around with you, and none of this helps at nighttime, or indoors.

So today we use clocks and watches.

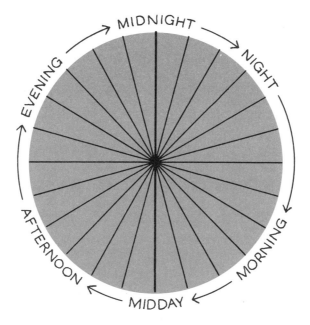

A day is the time from one sunup to the next sunup, daytime and nighttime. We divide one day into twenty-four pieces of time, 24 hours.

Some clocks have faces showing all 24 hours. The hand that shows the hours goes around exactly once every day.

Most clocks have faces showing 12 hours. For a 12-hour clock the hour hand goes around twice in a day, because there are two twelves in twenty-four (2 x 12 = 24).

One 12-hour period is from midnight to midday, called A.M. The other is from midday to the next midnight (called P.M.).

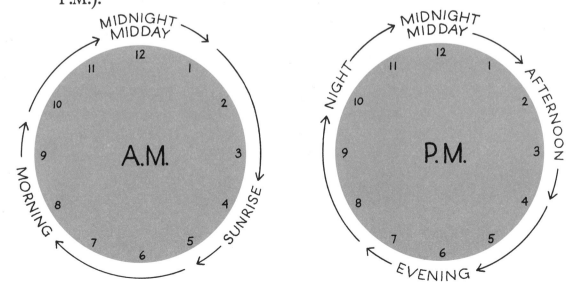

It is easy to tell the time when there is only one hand on your clock.

Gosh, I'm awake early. Nearly 6 A.M.

It's just past 9 o'clock.

Recess—halfway between 10 and 11 A.M.

It is noon on the dot. Time to eat lunch.

It is nearly 4 P.M. I'm going home.

TV time begins between 7 and 8.

I'm very sleepy—it's a bit past 9 P.M.

Make your own clock.

Take a paper plate, or use a round piece of cardboard. Also cut out a pointer. Put a hole in the center of the plate, and another at the blunt end of the pointer. Write numbers around the edge of the plate.

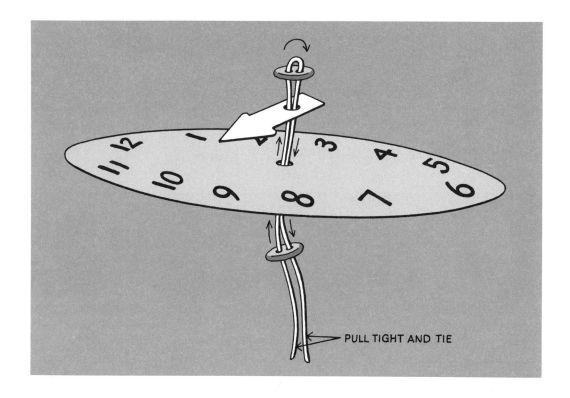

PULL TIGHT AND TIE

Get two buttons, bigger than the holes. Put string or thread through the buttons, pointer, and plate. Tie it off so that the hand moves around easily. Practice reading different times on your clock.

The hand of a clock can go around two ways. One way is called "clockwise," the other "counterclockwise" or "anti-clockwise."

Look at a real clock and watch to see which way is clockwise. Then find a jar or bottle with a lid that turns. Usually you turn the lid clockwise to tighten it.

What about the way a screw is tightened or an electric light bulb is turned in its socket?

As people learned more about clockmaking, they made clocks that measured an hour. The clockface was divided into small bits called minutes, and there were 60 of them.

The face of the minute clock looks like this. The hand goes all the way around its dial once while the hand on the hour clock just goes from one number to the next.

There isn't room to write numbers for all the minutes on a minute clockface. They would be too crowded. You can try to write all the numbers from 1 through 60 around a circle and see.

On most clockfaces you have to figure out the minutes. Some clockfaces show 5, 10, 15, 30, or 45 minutes past the hour, but you have to figure out the in-between minutes.

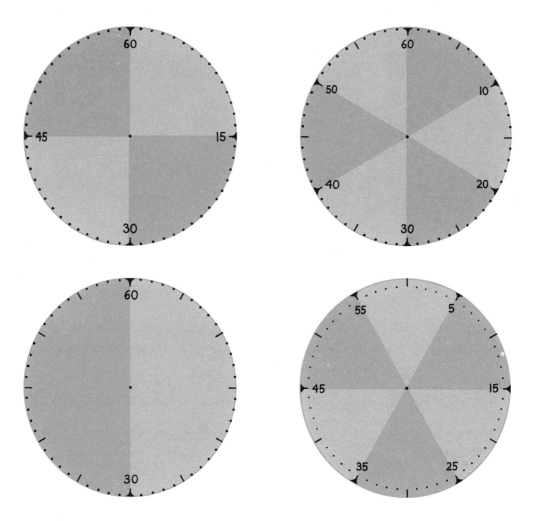

Make another face, for a minute clock. Use another paper plate and a longer pointer. Set the pointer, or hand, wherever you like and get a friend to read these times in minutes past the hour: 5 past, 10 past, 13 past, 27 past, 30 past, 37 past, 45 past, 59 past.

There is another way to read the minute hand.

"40 minutes past 8" can be called "20 minutes before 9" (Notice that $20 + 40 = 60$).

"50 minutes past 7" can be called "10 minutes before 8" ($10 + 50 = 60$).

"43 minutes past 10" can be called "17 minutes before 11" ($17 + 43 = 60$).

The "before numbers" are never written on clockfaces, though you could write them on your own. "5 minutes before" can be written 5b or ⁻5 ("negative 5"). The "before numbers" are similar to the other numbers but go counter-clockwise.

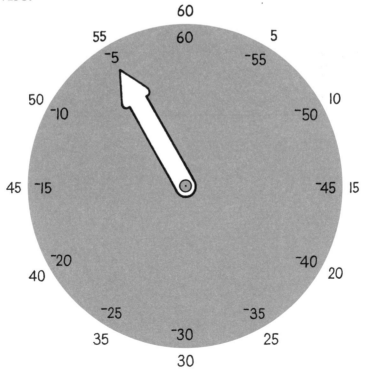

You are now ready to use your two paper clockfaces together.

If the hour hand looks like this the time is "just after 2."

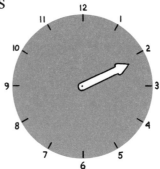

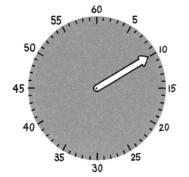

But if this minute clockface goes with it, the time is *ten* minutes past.   2:10.

About half past 2.

The minute hand tells us it is 28 minutes past 2.   2:28.

A bit before 3 o'clock.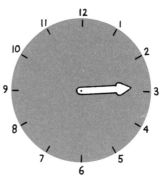

Exactly 52 minutes past 2, or 8 minutes till 3.   2:52. (We could write 3:-8, but no one ever does!)

3 o'clock.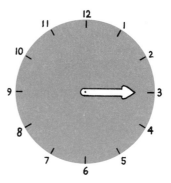

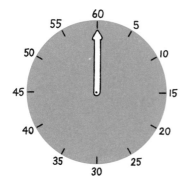

Exactly on the hour, on the dot!

On most clocks today both hour and minute hands are fixed onto the same dial. Around the clockface are marked all or some of the numbers 1 through 12 to show the hours. There are sixty dots around the edge to show the minutes.

For the hour time you look where the short hand points. For the minutes you use the long hand.

Eleven minutes past six.

6:11.

11 minutes after 6.

Six eleven.

We don't know whether it is morning time (A.M.) or afternoon (P.M.).

Seven forty-five.

7:45.

15 minutes before 8.

15 minutes till 8.

Or even, 45 minutes past 7.

Go and find a clock at home or in school. Draw it carefully. Put in the hands and the numbers. Watch the clock hands move a bit and make another drawing. Are both hands in different positions?

Make many drawings, again and again every few minutes. Take one complete hour on the job. You know when that is because the minute hand will be back in the same position it was in at the beginning of the hour.

Cut out each drawing. Shuffle them. Now try to put them in order again. Play with a friend. You could also write each time underneath. If you write it like this, 2:54, it is called the digital method.

Now see if you can find a real clock or watch whose hands can be moved easily. Check with a grown-up that it is all right for you to turn the hands yourself.

See what times you can tell.

Maybe you could set the hands at nine o'clock. Turn the hands slowly. Watch the minute hand pass through 1 minute past 9, 2 minutes past 9, 3 minutes past, and so on, until the hands show 10 o'clock.

Then ask someone else to set the hands. You try to tell the times they show.

Or try to set the hands like some of the clockfaces shown in this book.

Because there are four fifteens in 60 (4 x 15 = 60), we say that 15 is "one fourth" or "one quarter" of 60 (15 = ¼ of 60). This is also used in telling time.

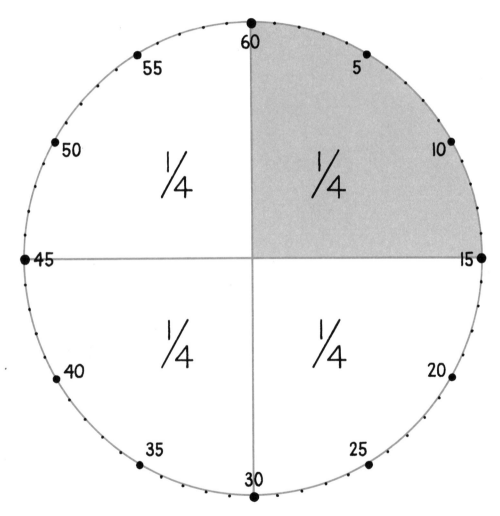

15 minutes is one quarter of an hour.

30 minutes is two quarters of an hour, or one half hour (2 x 30 = 60).

So you will hear people sometimes say:

"A quarter past three" for 3:15.

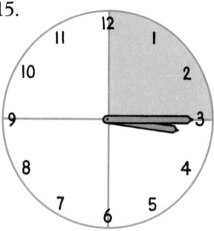

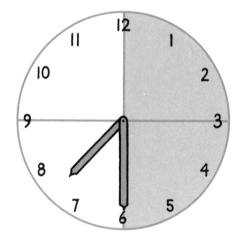

"Half past seven" for 7:30.

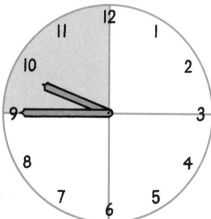

"A quarter to ten" for 9:45.

Even though 20 minutes is one third of an hour $(3 \times 20 = 60)$ and ⅓ of 60 = 20, no one says "one third past twelve" for 12:20.

For learning math, however, you could practice with all sorts of fractions of an hour: halves, thirds, fourths, fifths, sixths, tenths, twelfths, fifteenths, twentieths, thirtieths, sixtieths ($2 \times 30 = 60, 3 \times 20 = 60, 4 \times 15 = 60, 5 \times 12 = 60, 6 \times 10 = 60, 60 \times 1 = 60$).

¼ past 1   ⅔ past 9   ⁵⁄₁₂ past 11

quarter past 1   2 thirds past 9   5 twelfths past 11

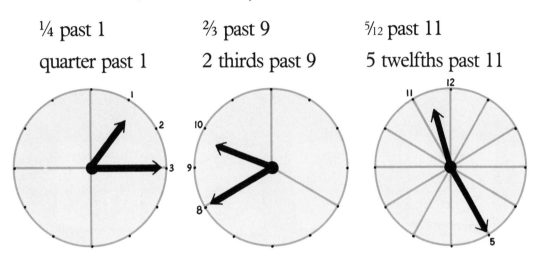

And can you read these clockfaces using fractions?

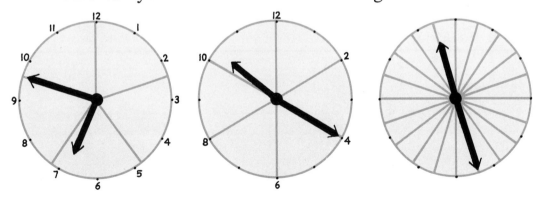

Can you make your clockface say ½ past 2, ⅚ past 7, ¹⁄₂₀ before 8?

Try some more games.

You and your friend draw 30 clockfaces on small cards showing different times. Copy them from a real clock.

Shuffle the cards. Now put them back into the order of times during one day. See if you can do this every time, using any card as the first.

Hold each card reflected in a mirror for your friend to read. Take turns. Take turns also in reading each card, saying "past" every time, and "till" every time, and the number of minutes every time.

In most houses there are dials like those on a clockface, but they don't tell the time, they tell how much gas or electricity a family has used. Find a meter inside or outside your house. The dials may look like this:

Some of the hands may go around counterclockwise and some may go clockwise. Notice that there are ten divisions on each face. You may be able to find someone to read this meter.

Time clocks could be divided into 10, and maybe one day astronauts will land on another planet, where the inhabitants count 10 hours in a day!

Try reading these unusual clockfaces.

This one is seen
in a mirror.

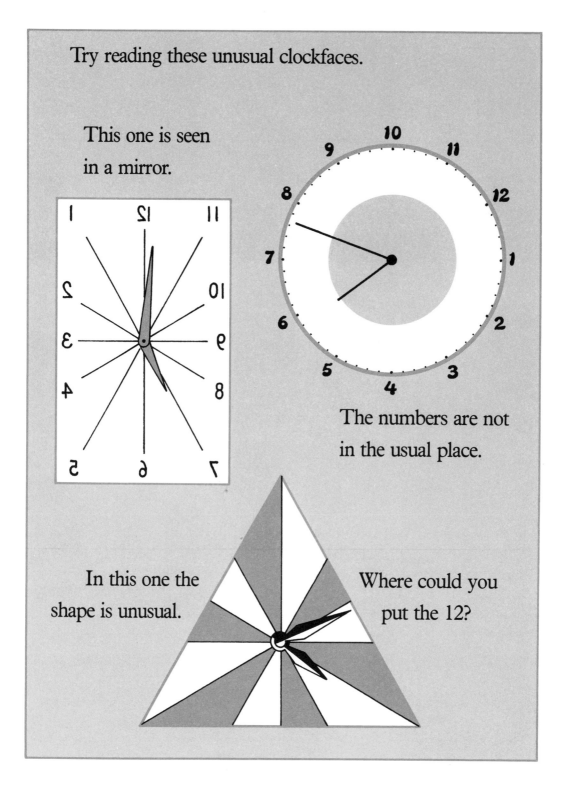

The numbers are not
in the usual place.

In this one the
shape is unusual.

Where could you
put the 12?

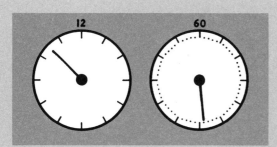

There are two separate dials.

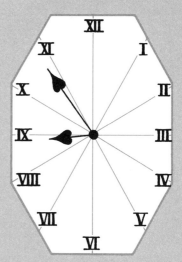

This one goes around
the other way.

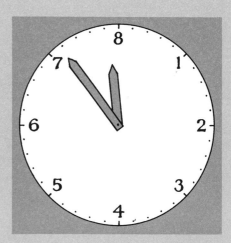

This is an 8-hour clock
with 40 minutes in an hour.

Here are some interesting things about clocks:

If a clock is running properly it will tell the right time all the time, but a clock that has stopped tells the right time, too, but only twice a day!

Do you know why?

If a clock runs too fast or too slow, it can be set at the right time, but it soon tells the wrong time again!

Do you know why?

Learning to tell time takes time. So be patient with yourself. You will learn in time to tell time, even if it seems confusing from time to time!